A New True Book

TROPICAL FISH

By Ray Broekel

*This "true book" was prepared
under the direction of
Illa Podendorf,
formerly with the Laboratory School,
University of Chicago*

 CHILDRENS PRESS, CHICAGO

Male swordtail

PHOTO CREDITS

Reinhard Brucker—cover, 31 (top right), 42, 45 (2 photos)

A. Kerstitch—2, 7, 9, 11, 12, 14, 15, 16 (top), 19, 21, 22, 23, 24, 25, 26 (2 photos), 28, 30, 31 (top left, middle, bottom left and right), 32, 33, 40, 41

James M. Cribb—4, 16 (bottom)

Carolina Biological Supply Company—20, 32, 35, 43

Marty Hansen—37, 39

Cover—Male Siamese fighting fish

Library of Congress Cataloging in Publication Data

Broekel, Ray.
  Tropical fish.

  (A New true book)
Previously published as: The true
book of tropical fish. 1956
    Includes index.
    Summary: Briefly describes the different kinds of
tropical fish and explains how to care for fish in an
aquarium.
    1. Tropical fish—Juvenile literature. 2. Aquariums—
Juvenile literature. [1. Tropical fish. 2. Aquarium
fishes. 3. Fishes. 4. Aquariums] I. Title.
SF457.25.B767 1983   639.3′4   82-19738
ISBN 0-516-01687-3   AACR2

86-1390

TABLE OF CONTENTS

Where Tropical Fish Come From. . . 5

How Tropical Fish Are Collected. . . 7

Live-Bearing Tropical Fish. . . 9

Egg-Laying Tropical Fish. . . 17

Your Pet Tropical Fish. . . 32

Words You Should Know. . . 46

Index. . . 47

WHERE TROPICAL FISH COME FROM

Some places in the world are warm all year round. They are called the tropics.

Parts of Central and South America are in the tropics. So are parts of Africa and Asia. There are also many tropical islands.

Many kinds of fish live in warm tropical waters. Some of these fish are small and colorful. They have babies often.

People like to keep small tropical fish as pets. Usually they keep these fish in aquariums. Almost 380 different kinds of tropical fish are kept as pets.

HOW TROPICAL FISH ARE COLLECTED

Sometimes tropical fish for pets are caught by people who live in the tropics. Sometimes people who sell tropical fish take trips to collect them.

Aquarium fish can be collected from tropical rivers, too.

Then the fish are taken to seaports or airports. They are shipped or flown to other places in the world.

Trains, trucks, and airplanes deliver tropical fish to many places. At last they reach the pet stores.

But sometimes tropical fish do not come from the tropics at all. They are raised in aquariums by dealers.

LIVE-BEARING TROPICAL FISH

Some tropical fish have babies that are born alive. Tropical fish that have their babies born alive are called live-bearers.

The guppy is a popular tropical fish. Guppies come

The female guppy is a live-bearing fish.

from the West Indies and South America.

They are important fish in these places. They eat many young mosquitoes. That keeps people from getting diseases mosquitoes carry.

But guppies make good pets, too. They are easy to take care of. They do not bother other fish.

Grown-up guppies are about one inch long. The female is gray. The male is many bright colors.

Guppies start having babies when they are three months old. During her life, one female can have fifty babies. Guppies are live-bearing tropical fish. So these babies are born alive.

Male guppy

Female swordtail (top) and male swordtail (bottom)

Swordtails are live-bearers, too. Their babies are born alive.

The male swordtail is a strange-looking tropical fish. A part of his tail fin really does look like a sword. The female swordtail does not have this sword.

Platy

The platy is another
live-bearer. Sometimes
platys are called moons.
There are many different
kinds of platys. They are
nice tropical fish to have
in an aquarium. They do
not fight with other fish.

Black mollie

Another popular tropical
fish is the black mollie.
Black mollies are also live-
bearers. Baby black
mollies are born alive.

Many people enjoy
keeping and raising live-
bearing tropical fish.

Both these fish are angelfish. The one shown below is a queen angelfish.

EGG-LAYING TROPICAL FISH

Some tropical fish have babies that are hatched from eggs. Tropical fish that have babies that are hatched from eggs are called egg layers.

Angelfish are egg-laying tropical fish. Baby angelfish hatch out of eggs.

There are several kinds of angelfish. Some live in salt water, such as warm parts of the Atlantic Ocean from Florida to Brazil.

Other angelfish live in fresh water, such as the Amazon River in South America.

Of course, you cannot put saltwater angelfish into fresh water or freshwater angelfish into salt water. If you did, they would die.

Angelfish have narrow bodies. Their long, pointed fins look a little like angels' wings. Grown-up angelfish are about the size of a silver dollar. Many people keep angelfish because they are so lovely and graceful to watch.

Angelfish

Zebra fish

Zebra fish are egg layers, too. They are striped somewhat like a real zebra. That is why they are called zebra fish.

Zebra fish never seem to rest. They move about very quickly.

Neon tetra

Neon tetras are colored
a bright, shiny red and
blue. That's how they got
their name. Neon tetras are
among the most beautiful
of the tropical fish.

Neon tetras are very small tropical fish.

Grown-up neon tetras
are very small. They are
smaller than guppies.

Baby neon tetras hatch
from eggs.

Tropical catfish

Tropical catfish come mainly from the countries in South America.

There are many kinds of catfish. They are also egg layers. Baby catfish hatch from eggs.

Catfish will not bother other fish. In fact, they help other fish.

Catfish are scavengers. Scavengers eat things that many other fish do not eat.

Catfish help keep an aquarium clean.

Catfish will eat food that has spoiled.

It takes some food a very short time to spoil in water. Most tropical fish will not eat food after it is spoiled.

Catfish, however, do eat spoiled food. That is why they make good aquarium fish. They help keep the aquarium clean.

The male Siamese fighting fish (above) will fight other male Siamese fighting fish (right). When they get excited, the males turn many different colors.

Some people like to
keep Siamese fighting fish
in their aquariums. These
little fish come from
around the Malay Archipelago.

Siamese fighting fish
have long, wavy fins. When
the male gets excited, he
turns red, blue, green, and
purple.

Only male Siamese
fighting fish battle each
other. One male will dart
at another and bite his
fins.

The male Siamese fighting fish helps care for its eggs.

The other male darts and bites back. The fish that gets exhausted first is the loser.

Male Siamese fighting fish will even attack their own reflections in a mirror.

You should never keep more than one male Siamese fighting fish in an aquarium.

But male Siamese fighting fish do other things besides fight. Siamese fighting fish are egg layers and the males help take care of the eggs.

First they blow a lot of bubbles. These bubbles stick together to make a nest. Then the male takes the eggs in his mouth and

Female Siamese fighting fish

blows them into the nest. There he watches them until they hatch.

Other egg-laying tropical fish are barbs, rasboras, danios, cichlids, and characins.

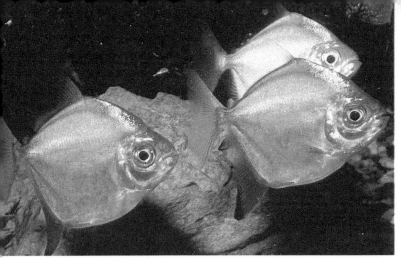

Top left: Characins
Top right: Rasbora
Left: Danio
Below left: Tiger barb
Below right: Cichlid

YOUR PET TROPICAL FISH

To have healthy tropical fish, you must put together the right kind of aquarium.

Fully equipped aquarium

Photograph by Carolina Biological Supply Company

Aquarium before water is added.

Use about two pounds of aquarium gravel for each gallon of water. Wash the gravel carefully.

Always let water you are going to use in your aquarium sit for at least twenty-four hours in a glass jar or an enamel pan.

This will let the chlorine gas rise out. Chlorine is a gas put into the water to kill germs. It helps people. But it will kill fish in an aquarium.

Fill the aquarium half full of water. Now put in your plants. Fish need plants to help them breathe.

Then carefully fill the aquarium to the top with water. Pour the water in slowly over your hand so it will not stir up the gravel.

Plants in an aquarium help the fish breathe.

Let your aquarium plants grow for at least one week before you put in any fish. A piece of glass placed on top of your aquarium will help keep dust out.

Place your aquarium in a spot where the plants will get enough light to stay green. Do not put your aquarium where it will get too much sunlight. If you do, tiny plants called algae will start growing.

A reflector will give off enough light to keep your water plants green. It also helps to keep the water warmer.

After a week check the temperature of the water

with an aquarium thermometer. Make sure the temperature is around 72 degrees.

Don't put too many fish into your aquarium. Give them lots of room so that they can grow into healthy fish.

Foil barbs (left) and black tetras (right)

If your fish are always at the top of the aquarium, you might have too many fish in it.

Feed your fish a little food two or three times a day. The food that would cover this spot O is about enough for three fish for one meal. A little tropical fish food will last for a long time.

Too much food can cause your gravel to turn black. Then the water will smell bad. You will have to clean your aquarium and start all over again.

Fish can go without food for days. So if you forget to feed them once in a while, it will not harm them.

Zebra fish

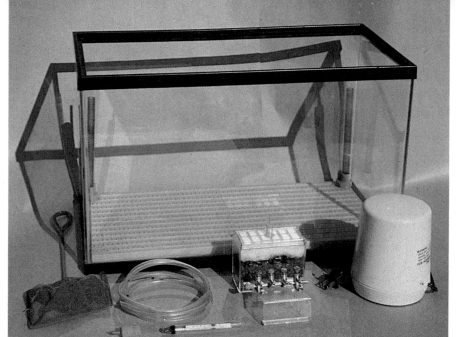

You can buy many
things to help you care for
your tropical fish.

Nets are handy when
you need to catch some of
your fish.

An air pump will help
put more oxygen into the
water and clean the water.

Reflectors help because the bulb inside the reflector gives off light. This light helps your plants grow. Algae usually will not grow under reflector light.

Custom-made home aquarium

Many different kinds of fish can be kept in an aquarium.

Photograph by Carolina Biological Supply Company

Close-up of tiger barbs

A thermostat heater
helps keep your aquarium
water at the temperature
you want.

Tropical fish are beautiful. They are interesting pets, too. Take care of tropical fish and see for yourself how much fun they can be.

Rosy barbs (above) and angelfish (below)

WORDS YOU SHOULD KNOW

algae (AL • jee) — organisms that do not have true roots, stems, or leaves

carbon dioxide (CAR • bun dye • OX • ide) — a gas made up of carbon and oxygen

charcoal (CHAR • kole) — a black material made by heating wood or other plant or animal matter

chlorine (klor • EEN) — a gas that is used to purify water

enamel (eh • NAM • il) — a smooth, hard coating that is baked onto surfaces to protect them

filter (FIL • ter) — a device used to pass air or water through it to clean out any dirt

gills (GILZ) — a body part with which fish and other water animals breathe

oxygen (OX • ih • jin) — a gas without color or smell that is part of the air and which people, animals, and plants need to live

reflector (re • FLEK • ter) — something that throws back light rays, heat, or sound

scavenger (SCAV • en • jer) — an organism that feeds on dead matter

siphon (SYE • fun) — a tube or pipe that is used to move liquid from one container to another

thermostat (THER • mo • stat) — a device that controls temperature automatically

tropic (TROP • ik) — the hot region of the earth near the equator

INDEX

Africa, 5
air pump, aquarium, 40
algae, 36, 41
Amazon River, 18
angelfish, 17-19
aquariums, 8, 25, 32-43
Asia, 5
Atlantic Ocean, 18
baby egg layers, 17, 22, 23
baby live bearers, 9, 11, 13, 15
barbs, 30
black mollies, 15
catfish, 23-25
Central America, 5
characins, 30
cichlids, 30
collecting tropical fish, 7, 8
danios, 30
egg-laying tropical fish, 17-30
fighting fish, Siamese, 27-29
food, 38, 39
food, spoiled, 25
freshwater angelfish, 18
gravel, aquarium, 33, 34, 38
guppies, 9-11
heater, aquarium, 43

light, for aquarium, 36, 41
live-bearing tropical fish, 9-15
Malay Archipelago, 27
moons (platys), 14
mosquitoes, eaten by guppies, 10
neon tetras, 21, 22
nest, Siamese fighting fish, 29, 30
nets, aquarium, 40
plants, aquarium, 35, 36, 41
platy, 14
rasboras, 30
reflector, aquarium, 36, 41
saltwater angelfish, 18
scavenger fish, 24
Siamese fighting fish, 27-29
South America, 5, 10, 18, 23
swordtails, 13
thermometer, aquarium, 37
thermostat heater, aquarium, 43
tropical catfish, 23-25
tropics, 5
water, aquarium, 33, 34, 36, 38, 40, 43
West Indies, 10
zebra fish, 20

About the Author

Ray Broekel is a full-time freelance writer who lives with his wife, Peg, and a dog, Fergus, in Ipswich, Massachusetts. He has had twenty years of experience as a children's book editor and newspaper supervisor, and has taught all subjects in kindergarten through college levels. Dr. Broekel has had over 1,000 stories and articles published, and over 100 books. His first book was published in 1956 (it was published by Childrens Press).